SUPER SCIENCE FEATS
THE INTERNET

by Nikole Brooks Bethea

Ideas for Parents and Teachers

Pogo Books let children practice reading informational text while introducing them to nonfiction features such as headings, labels, sidebars, maps, and diagrams, as well as a table of contents, glossary, and index.

Carefully leveled text with a strong photo match offers early fluent readers the support they need to succeed.

Before Reading

- "Walk" through the book and point out the various nonfiction features. Ask the student what purpose each feature serves.
- Look at the glossary together. Read and discuss the words.

Read the Book

- Have the child read the book independently.
- Invite him or her to list questions that arise from reading.

After Reading

- Discuss the child's questions. Talk about how he or she might find answers to those questions.
- Prompt the child to think more. Ask: Did you know how the Internet worked before you read this book? What else would you like to learn?

Pogo Books are published by Jump!
5357 Penn Avenue South
Minneapolis, MN 55419
www.jumplibrary.com

Library of Congress Cataloging-in-Publication Data

Names: Bethea, Nikole Brooks, author.
Title: The Internet / by Nikole Brooks Bethea.
Description: Minneapolis, MN: Jump!, Inc., [2018]
Series: Super science feats | "Pogo Books are published by Jump!" | Audience: Ages 7-10.
Includes bibliographical references and index.
Identifiers: LCCN 2017054670 (print)
LCCN 2017055689 (ebook)
ISBN 9781624968716 (ebook)
ISBN 9781624968709 (hardcover: alk. paper)
Subjects: LCSH: Internet—Juvenile literature.
Internet—History—Juvenile literature.
Classification: LCC TK5105.875.I57 (ebook)
LCC TK5105.875.I57 B4845 2018 (print)
DDC 004.67/8—dc23
LC record available at https://lccn.loc.gov/2017054670

Editor: Kristine Spanier
Book Designer: Michelle Sonnek

Photo Credits: Alexey Boldin/Shutterstock, cover (laptop); Nkuvshinov/Shutterstock, cover (screen); Shyamalamuralinath/Shutterstock, 1; Fotofermer/Shutterstock, 3; Pictorial Parade/Staff/Getty Images, 4; Bruce Dale/Getty Images, 5; Juice Images/Superstock, 6-7; Bettmann/Getty Images, 8-9; AFANASEV IVAN/Shutterstock, 10-11; ClassicStock/Alamy, 12-13; studioloco/Shutterstock, 14 (left); sirikorn thamniyom/Shutterstock, 14 (right); Evan Lorne/Shutterstock, 15; mirtmirt/Shutterstock, 16-17; Cressida studio/Shutterstock, 16 (cat); Denis Rozhnovsky/Shutterstock, 18; Carmen Murillo/Shutterstock, 18 (screen image); titoOnz/Shutterstock, 19; Andrey_Popov/Shutterstock, 20-21; Julian Rovagnati/Shutterstock, 23; Jason Winter/Shutterstock, 23 (code image).

Printed in the United States of America at Corporate Graphics in North Mankato, Minnesota.

TABLE OF CONTENTS

CHAPTER 1

INVENTING THE INTERNET

Why was the Internet invented? Scientists used to travel to access **data**. It was stored in many computers. Data could not be shared.

data

The scientists worried.
What if there was an
attack? What if data
was lost?

They wanted to link computers. How? They created a **network**. The year was 1969. Twelve years later, only 213 computers were on the network. But by 1995, 16 million people were online! **Servers** were developed to connect the networks.

DID YOU KNOW?

What was the first message sent between computers? Just two letters. LO. It should have read LOGIN. But the system crashed.

server room

Another network was made in the 1980s. It was for the fastest computers. Universities connected to them. Schools began teaching computer skills to students.

HTTP was developed next. It is a set of rules. For what? Sending data. This was the start of the World Wide Web.

DID YOU KNOW?

The World Wide Web is only one part of the Internet. It uses browsers. They access websites.

Search

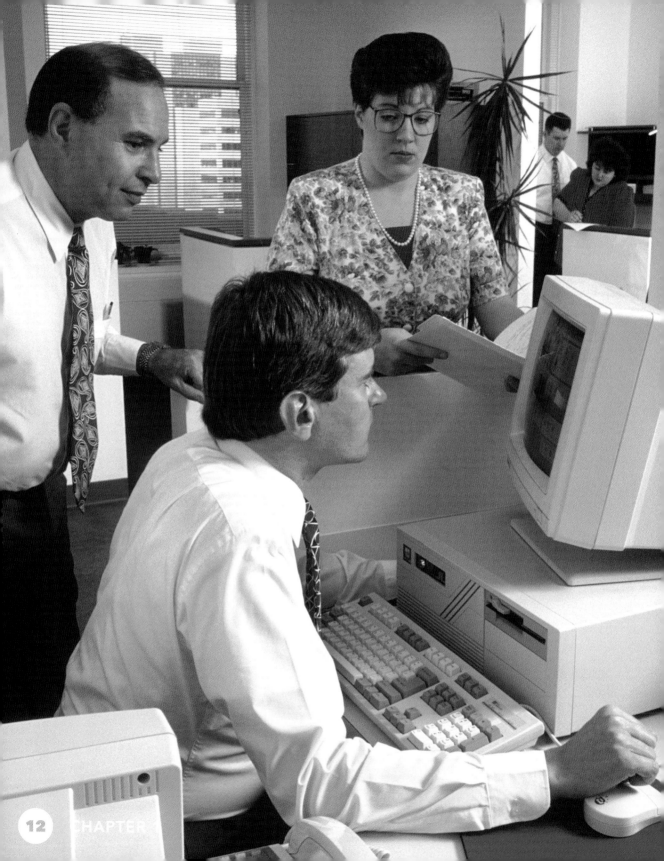

At first only researchers had access to the Internet. In 1993, it opened up to everyone. Companies had their own networks. **ISPs** formed. Anyone with a computer and a **modem** could go online. Use of the Internet exploded.

CHAPTER 2

HOW IT WORKS

The Internet is a network. Billions of computers access it. Who owns it? Nobody!

How do we connect to it? Modems. They connect to an ISP. Modems send data. They receive it. How? Through cables. **Fiber optic lines**. Or wireless signals.

modem

cable

Your ISP links to a close network. That network links to a national one. The high-level networks link to each other.

Retrieving data is easy. Start at a website. Click to view a photo. That photo is stored on a server. It is a large file. It is broken into small **packets**. Each packet is sent through the network. The photo reaches your screen. How fast? In less than one second!

TAKE A LOOK!

Data travels across the Internet in packets. If one pathway is too busy, a packet can travel a different route.

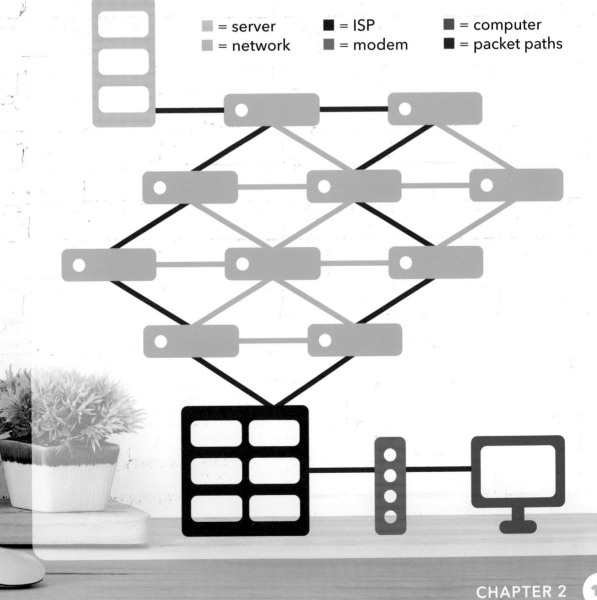

= server   = ISP   = computer
= network   = modem   = packet paths

CHAPTER 3

THE INTERNET AGE

Billions of e-mails are sent daily. Instant messages send across the world. But the Internet can do even more.

NASA tested the Internet in space in 2008. They sent images to a **spacecraft**. It sent data back. The Internet's reach hit a new level. It was 20 million miles (32.2 million kilometers) from Earth! One day we may be able to communicate with computers on other planets.

The Internet has changed the way we live. We can do many things online. We take classes. We play games. We read books. We shop. We chat with friends. How do you use the Internet?

ACTIVITIES & TOOLS

MAKE COMPUTER CODE

Computers do not read words like we do. Words must be encoded into binary numbers. This format has only two digits. We think of them as 1 and 0. Try encoding your name into binary numbers.

What You Need:

- paper
- pencil

ASCII Binary Alphabet Chart

Letter	Binary	Letter	Binary
A		N	
B		O	
C		P	
D		Q	
E		R	
F		S	
G		T	
H		U	
I		V	
J		W	
K		X	
L		Y	
M		Z	

❶ On the paper, write the first letter of your name.

❷ Find the letter in the ASCII Binary Alphabet Chart.

❸ Beside the letter on your paper, draw the eight squares that are next to the letter in the chart, coloring in the squares in the same sequence.

❹ Write the second letter of your name under the first and repeat the procedure.

❺ Continue until you have completed your entire name.

❻ Now replace each white square with a 1 and each black square with a 0.

❼ Your name is now encoded in binary digits.

GLOSSARY

data: Information collected in a place so that something can be done with it.

fiber optic lines: Lines that send information as light pulses along a glass or plastic strand.

HTTP: The set of rules that controls how data travels over the Internet. Short for hypertext transfer protocol.

ISPs: Companies that provide people with access to the Internet in exchange for a fee. Short for Internet service providers.

modem: An electronic device that allows computers to exchange data, especially over a telephone line.

NASA: Abbreviation of National Aeronautics and Space Administration, the government agency responsible for the civilian space program, as well as aeronautics and aerospace research.

network: A group of two or more connected computer systems.

packets: Small bits of data or information that have been broken down to send from one computer to another.

servers: Computers that process requests and deliver data to other computers on the network.

spacecraft: A vehicle that travels or is used in space.

INDEX

TO LEARN MORE

Learning more is as easy as 1, 2, 3.

1) Go to www.factsurfer.com

2) Enter "Internet" into the search box.

3) Click the "Surf" button to see a list of websites.

With factsurfer, finding more information is just a click away.